TYCHO
BRAHE

PIONEER OF ASTRONOMY

SPECIAL LIVES IN HISTORY THAT BECOME

Signature LIVES

TYCHO
BRAHE
PIONEER OF ASTRONOMY

by Don Nardo

Content Adviser: Martin Gaskell,
Professor of Astrophysics,
University of Nebraska

Reading Adviser: Rosemary Palmer, Ph.D.,
Department of Literacy, College of Education,
Boise State University

Compass Point Books ◈ Minneapolis, Minnesota

Compass Point Books
3109 West 50th Street, #115
Minneapolis, MN 55410

Visit Compass Point Books on the Internet at *www.compasspointbooks.com*
or e-mail your request to *custserv@compasspointbooks.com*

Editor: Anthony Wacholtz
Page Production: Bobbie Nuytten
Photo Researcher: Svetlana Zhurkin
Cartographer: XNR Productions, Inc.
Library Consultant: Kathleen Baxter

Art Director: Jaime Martens
Creative Director: Keith Griffin
Editorial Director: Nick Healy
Managing Editor: Catherine Neitge

Library of Congress Cataloging-in-Publication Data
Nardo, Don, 1947–
  Tycho Brahe : pioneer of astronomy / by Don Nardo.
     p. cm. — (Signature lives)
  Includes bibliographical references and index.
  ISBN-13: 978-0-7565-3309-0 (library binding)
  ISBN-10: 0-7565-3309-0 (library binding)
 1. Brahe, Tycho, 1546–1601—Juvenile literature. 2. Astronomers—
Denmark—Biography—Juvenile literature. 3. Astronomers—Denmark—
Biography—Juvenile literature. I. Title.

QB36.B8N37 2008
520.92—dc22   2007004608

SCIENTIFIC REVOLUTION

The Scientific Revolution was a period of radical change in basic beliefs, thoughts, and ideas. Most historians agree that it began in Europe about 1550 with the publication of Nicolaus Copernicus' astronomical theories about Earth and its place in the universe. It ended about 1700 with the landmark work of Isaac Newton and his resulting universal laws. During those 150 years, ideas about astronomy, biology, and physics, and the very way scientists worked, underwent a grand transformation.

Table of Contents

Chapter 1
TYCHO'S NEW STAR

❧❦❧

Fortunately for Tycho Brahe, the sky was clear on the evening of November 11, 1572. Otherwise, he would not have noticed the strange new visitor looming high above him as he walked to supper. The 25-year-old Dane had left his laboratory and walked briskly toward the main building of Herrevad Abbey. The quaint, old monastery was nestled in the countryside of Scania, a province of Denmark. Although Steen Bille, Tycho's uncle, was not a monk, he ran the abbey. He had allowed his nephew to live and do scientific research there.

Tycho had not yet decided which area of science to pursue. He was fascinated by the stars and planets and had considered becoming an astronomer, but he was equally drawn to alchemy. Alchemists were, in a

Tycho Brahe (pronounced TEE-ko BRA-hee) was a noted Danish astronomer.

sense, forerunners of modern chemists. At that time, the goals of alchemists included trying to change lead and other inexpensive metals into gold and searching for chemicals that might prolong human life.

As Tycho headed toward the abbey's main hall, something in the sky caught his attention. He later recalled:

Tycho turned parts of the Herrevad Abbey into what is now seen as the forerunner of a modern scientific research facility. The abbey had land that was worked by more than 300 farmers. It also featured extensive orchards, gardens, fish-ponds, a mill, and a large blacksmith's shop. Tycho added a lab stocked with chemicals for his alchemy experiments and a glassmaking shop to supply the containers he used in the lab.

> *I noticed that a new and unusual star, surpassing the other stars in brilliancy, was shining almost directly above my head; and since I had, from boyhood, known all the stars of the heavens perfectly, it was quite evident to me that there had never been any star in that place of the sky.*

The "place of the sky" Tycho was referring to was the constellation Cassiopeia. Situated not far from the Big Dipper, its stars form the vague outline of a woman sitting on a chair.

It was obvious to Tycho that the object shining so brilliantly above his head did not belong in Cassiopeia. In fact, it was so out of place that at first he was afraid it might be an illusion. He thought his eyes and mind

Tycho, who was always known by his first name, was entranced by the appearance of what he thought was a new star.

were playing tricks on him. So he hastily summoned some of the servants who worked at the abbey and asked them if they could see the object. To Tycho's delight, they could. "When I observed that others …

could see that there was really a star there," he later wrote, "I had no further doubts."

Having established that the strange heavenly visitor was real, the question for Tycho became: What could it be? He called it a star simply because it looked like one. But he was doubtful that a new star could suddenly appear in the sky because all of the scholars in his day accepted a different worldview. Nearly 2,000 years earlier, Aristotle believed that the stars are unchangeable. He also believed that the moon and planets move through the heavens but lie fairly close to Earth, the center of all things. Finally, he thought the stars lie far beyond the planets and do not move. Therefore, no new stars could appear and upset nature's balance.

Like other European scholars, Tycho had been brought up to accept these ideas about the heavens. So at first, he assumed the object was close to Earth, much closer than the moon. For a while, he considered that it might be a comet since they move through Earth's atmosphere. But Tycho quickly ruled out comets because the new object was bright and sharp, while comets look like fuzzy patches in the sky.

Eager to solve the mystery of the new star's true identity, Tycho observed it closely night after night for weeks. It eventually became brighter than the planet Venus, the brightest object in the night sky aside from the moon. For a few weeks, the new object was even

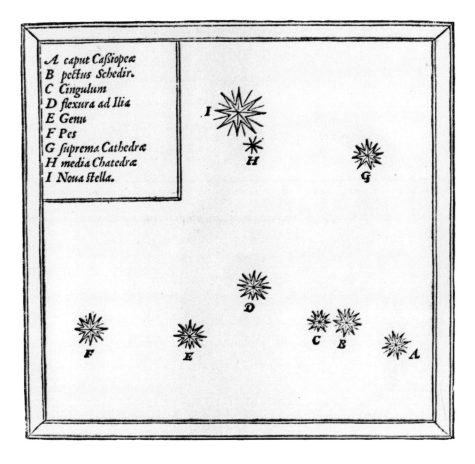

A caput Caſsiopeæ
B pectus Schedir.
C Cingulum
D flexura ad Ilia
E Genu
F Pes
G ſuprema Cathedræ
H media Chatedræ
I Noua ſtella.

visible in broad daylight. Over the course of about 16 months, however, it steadily faded. Then it disappeared as mysteriously as it had appeared.

During the time the object was visible, Tycho noted that it seemed to stay in the same spot in Cassiopeia. This ruled out the idea of a comet, since comets move steadily across the sky night after night. It also seemed to rule out the notion of it being a new planet, since planets also move through the sky. The

Tycho's drawing of the constellation Cassiopeia had the letter "I" marking the unknown celestial body.

object seemed to display the starlike traits of great distance and lack of motion.

But Tycho wanted to be sure, so he proceeded to measure the object's parallax. He knew that on Earth, the position of a distant object appears to shift when the person observing the object moves. For example, if one views a church steeple from one spot, certain scenery will be visible behind it. But when one walks a few hundred feet to one side, different scenery appears behind the steeple. Therefore, parallax is the apparent movement of an object caused by the observer's own movement.

Tycho was determined to identify the strange new celestial object.

Tycho knew that the closer an object is to an observer, the larger its parallax will be. A more distant object has a smaller parallax. So if the strange new object was relatively close to Earth, it would have a distinct and measurable parallax. Tycho measured the new star's parallax using a crude sextant, a device for sighting star positions. Each night, he measured the angle between the strange object and

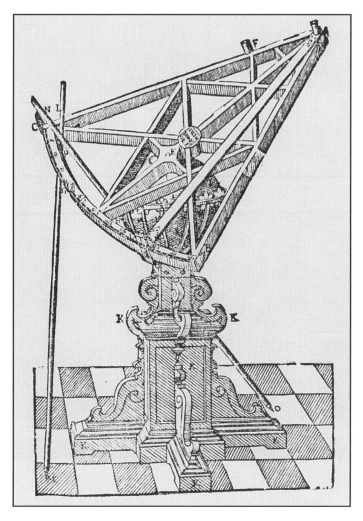

The sextant was one of many instruments Tycho used to study the sky.

several known bright stars.

As the weeks and months went by, he could find no parallax for the object. He concluded that the mysterious object did not move. He realized that it could mean only one thing: It had to be a distant star. The appearance of a new star in the heavens was, in

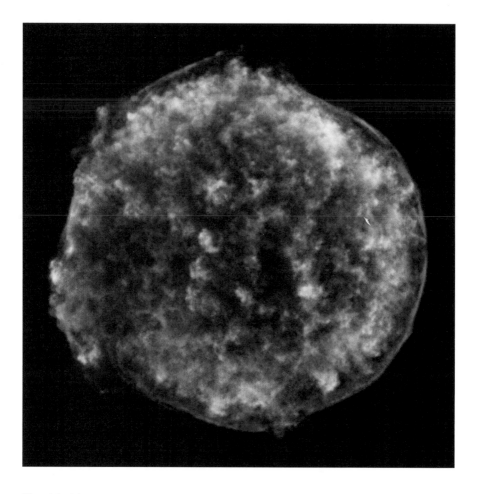

The object in the sky that Tycho had closely studied became known as Tycho's supernova. More than four centuries later, a powerful X-ray telescope photographed the remnant of the supernova.

Tycho's words, "a miracle, indeed, one that has never been previously seen before our time, in any age since the beginning of the world." What is more, it meant that the old worldview had been wrong—the distant heavens were *not* unchangeable.

Most other European scholars were not so quick to accept Tycho's findings, and they were certainly not prepared to question previous scientific authority on the word of a young, unproven scientist. They rejected Tycho's theory when he published a short book in 1573 titled *De Stella Nova,* meaning "The New Star." The object was not a star, Tycho's critics insisted. They argued that it was a comet or some other heavenly body. Tycho called such doubters "thick wits" and "blind watchers of the sky."

Though few people agreed with Tycho, his measurements of the new object and his book about it had made him famous. More important, these things had "put him on the path he was to follow for the rest of his life," according to his leading modern biographer, Victor E. Thoren. Thanks to the new star, Tycho decided to become an astronomer. He would soon find himself in charge of the most advanced astronomical observatory in the world. The data he would gather there would prove vital to the work of later pioneers of astronomy. ❧

Tycho coined a new term with the title of his book De Stella Nova. *Later astronomers came to use the word* nova *to describe a previously unknown star that suddenly appears in the sky. They eventually learned that the largest novae (plural for nova), called supernovae, are stars that explode. For a brief time, a supernova shines with the light of billions of normal stars. Tycho's supernova, which modern astronomers have called SN 1572, exploded about 20,000 years ago. It took that long for the light from the blast to reach Earth.*

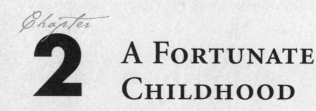2 A FORTUNATE CHILDHOOD

❧〜❧

At the time that Tycho Brahe studied the new star in Cassiopeia, he was already a wealthy man. He lived in comfort on the estate of Herrevad Abbey with servants to see to his personal needs. He had not acquired this position by years of hard work. Instead, Tycho had been born into one of Denmark's wealthiest families.

His father, Otte Brahe, was a nobleman with considerable influence in the Danish royal court. Otte had also inherited wealth and high position. Both of his grandfathers had been members of the Rigsraad, or Council of the Realm—an elite group that advised the king and often chose who would sit on the throne. Otte's father, Tyge Brahe, had also served in the Rigsraad before he died in battle.

Tycho learned all he could about astronomy as a student at the University of Leipzig in Germany.

In the wake of Tyge's passing, Otte inherited the family castle at Knudstrup, in the Danish province of Scania. Later he married Beate Bille, who also came from a wealthy, influential family. In their lofty stone fortress at Knudstrup, Tycho came into the world on December 14, 1546. His mother gave birth to 11 other children, but only seven of them survived infancy. It

Tycho was born at Knudstrup Castle in Denmark.

was common in those days for one-third or more of the children in large families to die young. There was a general lack of proper sanitation across Europe, and medicine was a primitive art. Among Tycho's siblings was a younger sister, Sophia. A bright and resourceful young woman, Sophia would later aid her brother in his scientific research.

When Tycho was 2 years old, his wealthy uncle, Jorgen Brahe, visited Knudstrup. It was only after Jorgen had departed that Otte and his wife noticed that something important was missing. Tycho later recalled that "without the knowledge of my parents," Jorgen took "me away with him."

Jorgen Brahe justified the kidnapping by pointing out that he and his wife, Inger, did not have any children. In his eyes, Otte and Beate had many children, so they should be generous and give one to their childless relatives. For reasons that remain unclear, Tycho's parents went along with this strange arrangement. Jorgen took Tycho to his estate at Tostrup, in eastern Scania, where, according to Tycho, his uncle "brought me up and thereafter supported me generously during his lifetime … and

Both of Tycho's homes, at Knudstrup and Tostrup, were in Scania (or Skane), a flat region with few forests or lakes. Today Scania makes up the southern part of Sweden. But in Tycho's time, the region was part of Denmark. The Danes lost Scania to Sweden in the Treaty of Roskilde in 1658, a half century after Tycho's death.

always treated me as his own son."

Uncle Jorgen was careful to see that Tycho, like other Danish children from wealthy families, was well educated. At the time, all of the elementary schools in Denmark were privately run. Most were run by churches, and the teachers were Protestant ministers. Tycho later remembered, "[I] was sent to grammar school in my seventh year." There he studied Latin and Greek, the Bible, and perhaps some elementary mathematics.

After finishing elementary school, fortunate young European noblemen almost always continued their education at a university. In April 1559, Tycho began attending the University of Copenhagen. Engraved above the front door of its main building were the words, "He looks up to the light of heaven." No one could have foreseen how fitting this phrase was, for young Tycho Brahe would grow up to be a world-famous observer of the heavens.

At first, astronomy was not Tycho's primary focus of study because his uncle wanted him to study law. Tycho also took courses in the liberal arts, which were taught in all European universities. These included geometry, arithmetic, logic, rhetoric, music, and Latin. Tycho eventually took an interest in astronomy, partly because the clergymen who ran the school strongly promoted it. They claimed that studying the heavens was a way to get closer to God.

However, it was a major celestial event that turned astronomy into a passion for him. On August 21, 1560, he observed a partial eclipse of the sun, which scholars had predicted would happen. That humans could

An eclipse was cause for great excitement for astronomers in the 1500s.

> *The liberal arts that Tycho studied were based on the ideas of two Roman scholars who had lived almost 1,000 years before. One was Cassiodorus, a civil servant who established a monastery in southern Italy in the year 540. The other was Martianus Capella, who wrote a popular encyclopedia. They advocated the teaching of mathematics, music, and astronomy, as well as Latin, Greek, and the Christian religion. Their writings were rediscovered during the European Renaissance and helped to shape the courses of study in European universities.*

foresee what was widely considered an act of God fascinated him. If an eclipse could be predicted, Tycho reasoned, perhaps other heavenly events could be predicted as well. Eager to try his hand at such predictions, he purchased two leading astronomy texts and pored over them whenever he had a chance. "By and by," he later wrote, "[I] got accustomed to distinguishing all the constellations of the sky."

When Tycho finished his courses in Copenhagen, he decided to continue his studies in Germany, a country that boasted some of the finest universities in Europe at that time. In February 1562, 15-year-old Tycho began attending the University of Leipzig. In addition to astronomy, he studied Latin, literature, and astrology. Astrologers claimed that the planets and stars affect the course of earthly events. Today astrology is considered to be a false science, but in Tycho's day nearly everyone, including scientists, believed it was based in reality. He even spent part of his time drawing up horoscopes for famous people.

Still, Tycho spent more time studying the night sky. Since telescopes had not yet been invented, all astronomical observations had to be done with the naked eye, aided by a few mechanical devices.

One of these was the radius, or cross staff. It consisted of two wooden bars connected at a right angle to form a cross. To measure the angle separating two stars, the observer held the radius so that one star was visible in a sight mounted on the crossbar.

Although Tycho used the cross staff to measure the distance between stars, the device could be used to measure the distance between any two objects.

Then a second sight was moved until the second star was visible through it. Numbers painted on the bars below the sights indicated the resulting angle.

However, Tycho found that these devices were clumsy and inaccurate. He realized that most of the professional star charts he studied were almost useless. "I've studied all available charts of the planets and stars and none of them match the others," he complained in 1563. He also wrote:

There are just as many measurements and methods as there are astronomers and all of them disagree. What's needed is a long term project with the aim of mapping the heavens conducted from a single location over a period of several years.

This idea would eventually become one of Tycho's main projects as an astronomer.

But for the moment, the young man could not consider tackling such a major project. For one thing, he had neither finished school nor had a chance to establish himself as a scientist. He did not even have an observatory to perform his experiments. There was also his family to think about. Both his father, Otte Brahe, and Uncle Jorgen disliked the idea of his becoming an astronomer. However, tragedy would soon claim the lives of both men, leaving Tycho to pursue his interests. ❧

3 A COSTLY DUEL

Tycho's life as a student at the University of Leipzig consisted of a never-ending flurry of activity. He was so busy with schoolwork in the daytime and celestial observations at night that he found little time for his family. But a tragedy occurred in June 1565 that forced him to make time.

In the winter of 1565, Uncle Jorgen and King Frederick II were riding their horses across a bridge when the king's horse suddenly reared up and threw him into the icy waters below. Jorgen left his horse and jumped in to save the king. King Frederick survived the ordeal, but the exposure to the freezing water left Jorgen with pneumonia, and he died shortly after. Tycho now found himself under the authority of his father, Otte.

Many of Tycho's portraits include a detailed depiction of his nose, a disfigurement resulting from a heated dispute.

Tycho had come to know his father during visits the young man had made to Knudstrup over the years. The two had formed a strong bond, yet they disagreed on some issues, particularly about Tycho's leanings toward science as a profession. Otte pointed out that astronomy was all right as a hobby, but he insisted that astronomers and other scientists were not much better than ordinary workers. He felt Tycho needed to quit school and choose a profession acceptable to members of the noble class, such as military officer, courtier, or diplomat.

However, Tycho refused to leave school. He told his father he had not yet made a firm decision about becoming an astronomer but wanted to keep that option open. In any case, he had a tremendous thirst for knowledge about the workings of the world and the universe.

Tycho was born in the latter years of the European Renaissance, an era in which a handful of scientists and other educated people were rejecting traditional ideas about the universe and humanity's place in it. In 1543, three years before Tycho's birth, Polish astronomer Nicolaus Copernicus proposed a controversial theory. The widely accepted notion that Earth lay at the center of the universe was wrong, Copernicus said. The sun and planets do not move around Earth. Instead, Earth is a planet that, along with the other planets, revolves around the sun.

As a student of astronomy, Tycho did not agree with Copernicus. In fact, most scientists had not yet accepted the notion of Earth as a moving planet. However, Tycho did not think that the astronomers of his day had all the answers. He was sure that much

Astronomers created their own theories by studying the sky and researching the writings of previous scholars.

about the universe remained undiscovered, and he was eager to resume his studies.

In April 1566, 19-year-old Tycho enrolled at the University of Wittenberg in eastern Germany. He had just begun his classes when an epidemic struck the town. In October, Tycho fled northward to Rostock, Germany, and entered the widely respected university there.

On the evening of December 10, 1566, he attended a party packed with members of the nobility. Many of those present, including Tycho, had too much to drink. He soon got into a heated argument with Manderup Parsberg, another Danish student who happened to be his third cousin. The two young men argued again at another party a few days after Christmas. Tycho, according to an eyewitness,

> *unexpectedly got into an argument with one of the table companions, and soon they were so wrought [worked] up ... they demanded swordplay of each other.*

In other words, they challenged each other to a duel. Although no accounts of the duel have survived,

Duels were fairly common among European aristocrats, but they turned out to be especially frequent in Tycho's family. In addition to his own duel in 1566, another of his third cousins slew a man in a sword fight in 1568. In 1581, one of Tycho's uncles killed a second cousin the same way. One of Tycho's first cousins died in a duel in 1584, as did another uncle, Peder Rud, in 1592.

Parsberg got the upper hand and managed to slice off most of Tycho's nose. Fortunately for Tycho, infection did not set in. If it had, he might have lost more of his face or even died. Wondering what he should do about his terrible disfigurement, he finally decided to wear false noses made of metal. He reportedly had a goldsmith fashion several realistic substitutes from gold and silver.

Duels were commonly used to settle disputes in the mid-1500s.

Tycho was enrolled at the University of Rostock, Germany, when he lost his nose in a duel.

Hoping to test the accuracy of this account, medical experts opened Tycho's tomb in 1901 and examined his remains. They found green stains around his nasal area, which means that some of his

false noses were made of copper. Therefore, it may be that he wore heavy gold or silver noses for formal occasions and donned lighter, more comfortable copper ones the rest of the time.

The duel that cost Tycho his nose also caused him to quit his studies at Rostock. University authorities demanded that he pay a fine for dueling on school property. Unwilling to do so, he left the university. In the late 1560s, Tycho traveled around Europe, learning whatever he could about astronomy and alchemy. Although he kept in touch with his family in Scania, he did not visit Knudstrup very often, perhaps hoping to avoid arguing with his father. Every chance he got, Otte Brahe tried to discourage his son from becoming a scientist.

However, in December 1570, Tycho received a letter from his siblings informing him that their father was very ill. It was clear to the family that it would be Otte's last Christmas. So Tycho hurried home and stayed until his father died on May 9, 1571. In a letter to a friend a few days later, Tycho described Otte's death. The words revealed

> *Tycho chose false noses that were made of metal and painted to resemble skin tones. But he did have another option—a medical technique that first came into use in Europe when he was in his 30s. An Italian surgeon, Gasparo Tagliacozzi (1545–1599), pioneered the medical art of plastic surgery. Working in Bologne, Italy, he performed skin grafts to repair facial wounds and injuries, including lost noses. It remains unknown why Tycho did not seek Tagliacozzi's services.*

Tycho temporarily set aside his astronomy studies after finding out that his father was near death.

his genuine feelings for his father as well as Tycho's strong devotion to Christian beliefs. He mentioned his "distress and great sorrow over my father's departure from this life." Then he added:

> *My father passed from this wretched life of mortality so peacefully and quietly to the heavenly and eternal realm of our father [God]. ... He said farewell to her [his wife] and entrusted her to us children and his friends. Then he shut his eyes again and listened to the priest's words of consolation.*

The contents of Otte Brahe's will revealed how much he had cared about his son. Tycho not only inherited a large share of the Knudstrup estate, but every year he was also to receive a hefty income from 200 farms, 25 rented cottages, and five grain mills.

With this vast wealth, Tycho would be able to pursue whatever scientific studies and experiments he pleased. At last he would have his own laboratory and maybe even an observatory. For the moment, such facilities would need to be near Knudstrup so he could visit his grieving mother on a regular basis. His uncle Steen's invitation to move to nearby Herrevad Abbey was therefore extremely welcome. It was there, in 1572, that Tycho would observe the new star in Cassiopeia and launch his career as an astronomer.

Chapter
4 A LAVISH HOME LIFE

❦

Moving to Herrevad Abbey and studying the new star in Cassiopeia were not the only activities that kept Tycho busy. In his late 20s, he started a family and created a settled home life. As the years went on, his home life became increasingly complex and lavish. He was a very wealthy man, and he came to know the Danish king, receiving favors and gifts from him from time to time.

In addition to his grand lifestyle, Tycho displayed some strange personal habits and tastes. These earned him a reputation as an eccentric, or odd, individual. Along with his scientific genius, his traits and lifestyle made him seem larger than life.

Around 1571, Tycho fell in love with a young woman named Kirsten Jorgensdatter, the daughter

Wealthy people displayed their high status by filling their homes with expensive furniture and decorations.

of a minister in Knudstrup village. The problem was that she was a commoner. Members of nobility were expected to marry someone from their own social class. Marriages between members of different classes did exist, but as a rule, society disapproved of them.

This disapproval was reflected in Danish law. A noble man and common woman who had a relationship were forbidden to have a formal marriage ceremony. If they lived together for three years, they were legally married, but the woman remained a commoner and could not enjoy the status and privileges of a noble. Moreover, any children the couple had were considered commoners. They could not inherit their father's status or property. Thus, in starting a family, Tycho made himself, his wife, and his children social outcasts from the noble class. One of his students later said, "All of Tycho's relatives were very disturbed by the diminished esteem the family suffered because of Kirsten's low birth."

Tycho's family and the rest of society were soon forced to accept Kirsten because of his new friendship with King Frederick II. After Tycho's book, *De Stella Nova*, appeared in 1573, he became a recognized authority on the heavens. In the years that followed, he gave lectures about astronomy. He also constructed several instruments for studying the sky and gathered students who wanted to learn from him. The king received many favorable reports

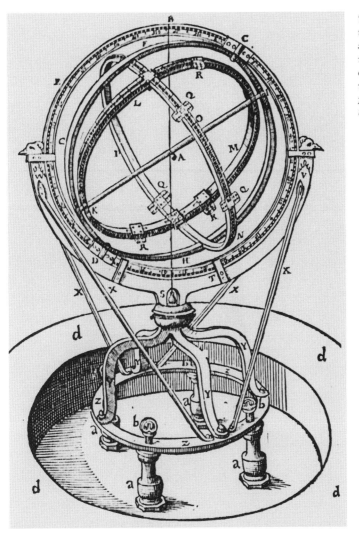

The armillary was one of several instruments Tycho constructed to measure the positions of the stars.

about these activities. Tycho's research could greatly benefit Denmark, Frederick reasoned. They could make the country seem like a land of great learning and wisdom.

In February 1576, Frederick offered to provide

King Frederick II realized the potential of Tycho's research and eagerly offered to fund his ongoing work.

financial support and other help for Tycho's work. He gave Tycho an entire island, known as Hven (or Ven), near Scania's western coast. He also paid for the building of a castle and large observatory there and provided Tycho with workmen and servants. The king told Tycho:

There you can live peacefully and carry out the studies that interest you, without anyone disturbing you. ... You who belong to a family which has always been dear to me, and you who are said to have considerable insight into such matters [the workings of the heavens]. I see it as my duty to support and promote something like this.

Tycho, at the age of 29, eagerly accepted the king's generous offer. Not only would he have all the instruments, helpers, and other means necessary to study the heavens, but as King Frederick's friend and client, he would also be socially accepted. No one would dare criticize his wife and children for their social status.

Tycho only had one child, a 2-year-old daughter named Magdalene, when he acquired Hven in 1576. (His first daughter, Kirstine, had died that year at age 3.) Magdalene and her mother remained at Knudstrup for a few years while Tycho oversaw construction of the castle on Hven. He traveled back and forth whenever possible to spend time with his growing family. Three more daughters—Sophie, Elisabeth, and

On May 23, 1576, Denmark's King Frederick II made the transfer of Hven Island to Tycho official. The royal decree stated: "To our beloved Tyge [Tycho] Brahe [I give] our land of Hven, with all our and the crown's tenants and servants who live thereon, and with all the rent and duty which comes from it ... to have, enjoy, use, and hold; free and clear, without any rent, all the days of his life."

Cecile—were born in 1578, 1579, and 1580, respectively. (A baby boy, Claus, lived only a few days after his birth in 1577. Tycho never saw him.)

The family moved into the finished castle in November 1580, after which Tycho and Kirsten had two sons. Tycho Jr. was born the following year, and Jorgen was born in 1585.

Other people besides family members lived around Tycho on Hven. Some of them were student-assistants, young men who dreamed of becoming astronomers. Each year, Tycho provided several of them with room and board. In exchange, they helped him with his research, learning much in the process. In addition, maintaining the castle and other buildings on the island required the services of numerous people. These included cooks, bakers, butlers, maids, gardeners, blacksmiths, farmers, fishermen, nannies for the children, and various craftsmen.

However, the workers were not always happy about providing these services. Evidence shows that Tycho was a very demanding boss, and he sometimes mistreated the island workers. He often forced

Building the main house and other facilities on Tycho's estate on Hven required the labor of hundreds of workers. Many of them did almost nothing but dig for years on end. The huge hole for the foundation of the main house alone took several months to dig. Other workers dug clay from pits to make the bricks to construct the house and other buildings. In addition, Tycho ordered the digging of more than 60 fishponds.

ORTHOGRAPHIA PRÆCIPVÆ DOMVS ARCIS VRANIBVRGI in Infula Porthmi Danici Venufia, *vulgo* Huenna, Aftronomiæ inftaurandæ gratia, circa annum MDLXXX. à TYCHONE BRAHE exædificatæ.

Tycho's castle and observatory at Hven

them to work without pay, for instance. Also, anyone who did not work hard enough or broke a rule was punished. Tycho maintained a dungeon where he locked up unruly workers for days or weeks, depending on the severity of their offenses. This dungeon can still be seen today.

Whether happily or reluctantly, the workers saw to every one of Tycho and Kirsten's needs, no matter how small. One need that Tycho viewed as important was to have proper entertainment during family meals. Never a small affair, a typical lunch or dinner featured at least two dozen people. They sat at an immense oak table in the castle's dining hall, which Tycho named the Winter Room. In addition to his immediate family, Tycho would also invite his student-assistants and other guests to the gathering. Both during and after the meal, the diners enjoyed the performances of singers, dancers, jugglers, and acrobats.

There was also a jester on hand during the dinners. Jesters told jokes and spouted witty comments on current events. According to some accounts, one of Tycho's jesters was a dwarf named Jeppe. Tycho thought Jeppe had psychic powers. In one incident, Tycho ordered two of his assistants to sail to the mainland on an errand. Jeppe then

Jesters were clownlike entertainers who could be found in many of the royal and wealthy households in Europe.

exclaimed, "See how your folk wash themselves in the sea!" Soon afterward, Tycho learned that the boat had sunk, forcing the two assistants to swim to shore. It was also reported that Jeppe sat under the table during family meals and sometimes ate scraps of food Tycho tossed to him.

Another member of Tycho's family on Hven was his pet elk. Tame and friendly, the enormous animal roamed freely throughout the castle and the grounds. It had a tragic end, however. Someone fed it beer, making it drunk and causing it to fall down a flight of stairs and die. It is unclear where Tycho was when this unfortunate incident occurred, but he was most likely working in one of the island's two observatories, which were by far the world's largest and best-equipped. ૭৯

ATLAS COELESTIS,
seu
HARMONIA
MACROCOSMICA

5 MAGNIFICENT OBSERVATORIES

❧

Tycho called his new castle on the island Uraniborg. He named it after one of the Muses—a group of minor goddesses in ancient Greek mythology that oversaw the arts and sciences. Urania was the goddess of astronomy. It was said that she could predict the future through the positions of the stars. To Tycho, who was fascinated by the ever-changing view of the heavens, using Urania as his home's namesake seemed especially appropriate.

Uraniborg was more than a residence with ample quarters for Tycho's family, assistants, and guests; it was also a scientific institution. It had a large-scale alchemy lab equipped with several ovens and thousands of glass containers. The house also featured one of the two astronomical observatories Tycho

A 17th-century painting depicts Urania, the muse of astronomy, surrounded by (from left) Tycho, Ptolemy, St. Augustine, Copernicus, Galileo, and Andreas Cellarius, all important astronomers of their time.

constructed on Hven. In addition, there was a large library, and in a massive open space in the center of the building loomed what one eyewitness described as "a fountain with a water-carrying figure rotating around and throwing water into the air in all directions."

The exterior of Uraniborg was no less imposing and complex than its interior. Dozens of chimneys, arches, domes, and spires projected upward from the rooftops. The great house rested inside an enormous square bounded by a wall 18 feet (5.5 meters) high, made of earth and stone. The four corners of the square pointed to the four cardinal directions—north, south, east, and west. A number of smaller buildings rose within the square. Among them were quarters for the maids, cooks, and other servants who worked in the main house. There was also a printing shop that created pamphlets and books describing Tycho's work and discoveries.

The centerpiece of Uraniborg was Tycho's main observatory, which he called the Museum. The Museum contained star charts, books, globes

Tycho believed many of the existing publishers in Denmark were unreliable. In 1584, he established his own press on the grounds of Uraniborg. His first printer, known only as Joachim, stayed a year or two and was succeeded by Christopher Weida. Over the years, Weida published several books about astronomy, including some of Tycho's own observations. The Uraniborg press also published some of Tycho's poetry.

representing the heavens, and mechanical instruments. Tycho and his assistants spent many hours in this chamber planning and discussing their observations. These observations took place on two terraces above the Museum, where Tycho and his aides could see the night sky without mountains or trees obstructing their view.

Tycho's Museum and observation decks contained numerous instruments designed to study the sky. He bought a few of them, but he designed most of them himself and paid the finest craftsmen in Europe to

Tycho's observatories provided a clear vantage point to view the entire sky.

build them. Tycho took particular pride in his great sky globe, which was completed late in 1580. A sphere measuring 5 feet (1.5 m) in diameter, it was covered in brass plates and represented the night sky. The globe had movable metal circles running around its surface that allowed Tycho to follow and record the changing positions of the planets. To chart the exact

Tycho recorded the exact positions of more than 700 stars on his great sky globe.

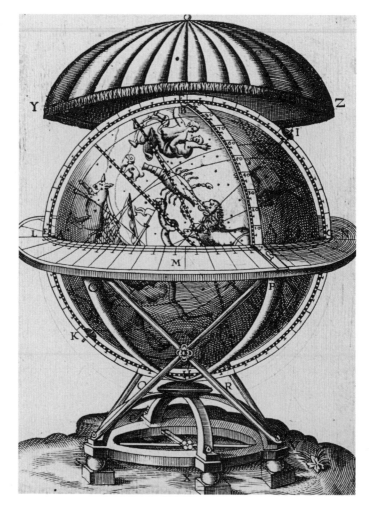

position of a star, he painted a dot representing that star on the globe.

Another instrument Tycho used—the armillary—was also shaped like a sphere. Unlike his globe, however, it had no solid surface. Instead, the armillary consisted of several large, movable metal rings forming the "skeleton" of a globe. Numbers indicating degrees in the sky were painted onto the edges of the rings. (An imaginary curved line stretching across the sky from the northern horizon to the southern horizon contains 180 degrees.) By lining up the armillary's rings in various ways, he could measure star positions.

The armillary was invented well before Tycho's era. However, he created the finest versions ever built up to that time, including one finished in 1581 that was the same size as his great globe. But Tycho, who wanted the most accurate measurements possible, was not satisfied with this new instrument. He felt it did not measure the positions of heavenly bodies accurately enough. So he got to work and in 1585 introduced a new, larger, and more accurate armillary. This version, which lined up with Earth's equator, was 10 feet (3 m) across.

Tycho achieved still more accurate measurements with some of the quadrants he designed. A quadrant, which means one-quarter, was an instrument featuring a wooden or metal framework shaped like a pie

*The quad-
rant was an
improvement
from the radius
Tycho had used
when he was
younger.*

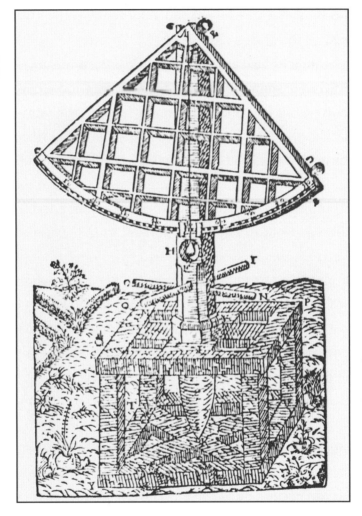

slice. The quadrant's framework covered 90 degrees,
or one-fourth of a full circle.

In some ways, the quadrant worked like the radius,
the crosslike measuring device Tycho had used in
his youth. The observer sighted two distant objects
through sights, or holes, on the quadrant's rim and

measured the angle between the sights. Tycho's quadrants were much more reliable than a radius, however. He attached each of his quadrants to a heavy base that kept the instrument from jiggling. He also installed more accurate sights. These efforts demonstrate how important achieving accuracy was to Tycho.

With his sky-measuring instruments, Tycho's Museum was a magnificent facility. However, each year he accumulated more instruments, and many of them were quite large and took up a great deal of space. By the end of 1583, the Uraniborg observatory had become too crowded. Tycho decided to build a second observatory about 100 feet (30 m) outside the castle's south wall. Work began in the spring of 1584, and the new building was finished two years later. Tycho called it Stjerneborg, Danish for "star castle."

The new observatory was at ground level, and the largest instruments lay inside circular sheds to protect them from wind and cold. Each shed was topped by a dome that rotated by a cleverly designed mechanism. As Tycho himself

In 1583, Tycho finished work on the largest astronomical instrument he ever designed. Called a triquetrum, it consisted of three wooden or metal arms connected by hinges. The arms moved, so one could adjust them to form triangles of various shapes and sizes. Using sights mounted on the instrument, one could measure the height of a star, planet, or comet from the horizon. The main arm of Tycho's triquetrum was about 11 feet (3.4 m) long, and the entire device weighed half a ton or more.

N
W · E
S

0 _____ 30 yards
0 _____ 30 meters

Uraniborg

Observatory

Observatory

Observatory

Living Quarters

Observatory

Observatory

Observatory

Øresund

N
W · E
S

Hven

◙ *main map*

Øresund

0 _____ 1 mile
0 _____ 1 kilometer

Stjerneborg

Observatories

Most of the space in Tycho's two castles was reserved for the observatories.

recorded, it consisted of a series of wheels hidden in a track at the dome's bottom edge. He wrote:

> With the aid of these wheels, the roof
> (could) be turned around with little effort.
> ... In this way, the two oblong windows
> which (were) placed in the roof [dome]
> opposite each other ... (could) be turned
> toward any star that was to be observed.

This mechanism was the forerunner of those used in the domes of observatories built in later centuries.

In a central position among Stjerneborg's sheds, Tycho's workmen constructed a chamber slightly below ground level. Reached by a staircase, it was called the warming room. It gave Tycho and his assistants a place to warm up every hour or two on cold nights, especially during Denmark's harsh winters.

Above the main entrance to the Stjerneborg compound, Tycho placed a sign that read: "Neither wealth nor power, but only knowledge, alone, endures." The moment the facilities began operating, Tycho and his aides began collecting reams of data. Later generations of astronomers would use this information to form an increasingly accurate picture of the heavens. ᴓ

6
A VISION OF THE HEAVENS

With his advanced instruments and observatories on Hven, Tycho had a huge advantage over other astronomers of his day. Most of them still used the more primitive radius, or they simply had fewer, smaller, and less-accurate instruments. In addition to having the best equipment, Tycho was a brilliant thinker and tireless worker.

The combination of these factors resulted in a major achievement between 1577 and the early 1590s: Tycho introduced a new and daring vision of the structure of the heavens. His cosmic model contradicted that of the old worldview, which had been accepted for nearly 2,000 years. The model of the heavens introduced by Copernicus had also challenged the traditional views. But most astronomers still did not accept Copernicus' claim that Earth circles the sun.

Part of the reason for this reluctance was religious belief. Astronomers, including Tycho, were devout Christians who adhered to the teachings of their faith. Priests and other theologians cited various passages in the Bible that seemed to indicate that Earth does not move. Also, various measurements Tycho made over the years appeared to confirm a stationary Earth. As he himself once put it, Earth was a "hulking, lazy body, unfit for motion."

In 1577, a dramatic event made Tycho begin to doubt the traditional cosmic model and formulate his own. On the evening of November 13, he was sitting beside one of his newly dug fishponds on Hven. Hoping to catch something for supper, he was probably not thinking about stars, planets, or other celestial bodies. He happened to glance at the darkening western sky, and he caught sight of a bright, somewhat hazy object that clearly did not belong. As the sky grew still darker, he saw that it had a faint tail. Tycho realized he was looking at a bright comet.

Most Renaissance scholars, including Tycho, rejected Copernicus' claim that Earth revolves around the sun. However, Tycho and the others did realize that Earth is a sphere. This had been known since the time of Aristotle and other ancient Greek thinkers. In the 1300s, for instance, the Italian mathematician Nicole Oresme wrote: "The earth is round like a ball and ... is at the centre of the Universe." Thus, the popular modern belief that medieval people thought Earth is flat is incorrect.

Excited by the new cosmic visitor, Tycho began studying it intensely. On every clear night, he carefully observed its motion across the sky until it disappeared from view in January 1578. He also took careful measurements using the quadrants and other instruments on the island.

At first, Tycho expected his measurements to show that the comet was relatively close to Earth's surface. After all, the old worldview maintained that comets exist between Earth and the moon. But nearly every test Tycho conducted showed that the comet was far beyond the moon. Eventually, he

After studying the movements of a comet, Tycho began to doubt the common beliefs about the structure and workings of the universe.

concluded that the object was located about 150 Earth diameters (about 1.2 million miles, or 1.9 million km) away. Moreover, the comet was not orbiting Earth, as the traditional cosmic model predicted it should.

Tycho realized that his observations clearly disproved the traditional views. First, the idea that comets existed inside Earth's atmosphere had been wrong. The belief that all heavenly bodies revolve around Earth was also in error.

Tycho's thorough research debunked many of the traditional ideas.

In addition, the comet's motion seemed to show that the Greeks were mistaken on another point: that a series of huge invisible spheres floated in the sky.

They had believed that the spheres nested inside one another, with Earth lying in the center. Each sphere carried along a different celestial object—the sun, moon, or a planet—on its surface. According to the old worldview, these objects always remained attached to their respective spheres, and nothing could pass through or between the spheres.

However, Tycho's measurements indicated that the comet of 1577 had moved right through the spheres of several planets. From this, he concluded that the old worldview had been wrong and that no such spheres existed. But if so, what kept the planets moving along in their orbits? This inspired Tycho to begin a careful and painstaking study of the movements of the planets and other heavenly bodies. He became determined to produce a new model of the heavens to replace the traditional one. The project occupied much of his time on Hven between 1578 and 1587.

The idea of giant, invisible spheres carrying the heavenly bodies through the sky originated with ancient Greek astronomers. Pythagoras (sixth century B.C.) and his followers held that three cosmic spheres existed. Later, Eudoxus (fourth century B.C.) upped the number of spheres to 27. His younger contemporary, Aristotle, declared that 55 cosmic spheres existed. It was Aristotle's view that remained widely accepted until the 1500s and 1600s.

After taking thousands of measurements over these years, Tycho published his new cosmic model in 1588. The book it appeared in was titled *Concerning the New Phenomena in the Ethereal World.* (By *ethereal,* he meant heavenly or cosmic.) He named his unique vision of the heavens the Tychonic model.

Tycho acknowledged that Copernicus was right to say that the planets move around the sun, not Earth. However, Tycho felt it would be going too far to remove Earth from the center of things. He could find no evidence that Earth moved in any way. Instead, he achieved a middle ground between the two views. Tycho succeeded, in his own words, in "expounding [describing] the motions of the planets according to the models ... of Copernicus, but reducing everything to the stability of the Earth."

In Tycho's cosmic model, therefore, Earth remained immovable at the center of the universe. The sun moved around Earth, and at the same time, the planets and comets revolved around the sun. In this way, as Tycho saw it, the sun carried most of the heavenly bodies around Earth. That gave people the impression that these bodies orbited Earth directly.

Tycho had no sooner put these ideas on paper when he was jolted by troubling news. Another astronomer, Nicholas Baer—better known as Ursus—had also published a book in 1588. Ursus presented basically the same cosmic model as Tycho's. The difference was that Ursus' version was less comprehensive and cited few celestial observations as proof. It was immediately clear to Tycho and his assistants

Copernicus' idea of a sun-centered universe was not accepted until long after his time.

that Ursus had stolen the idea from them. They pointed out that Ursus had worked at Uraniborg for a few months in 1584. At that time, Tycho charged,

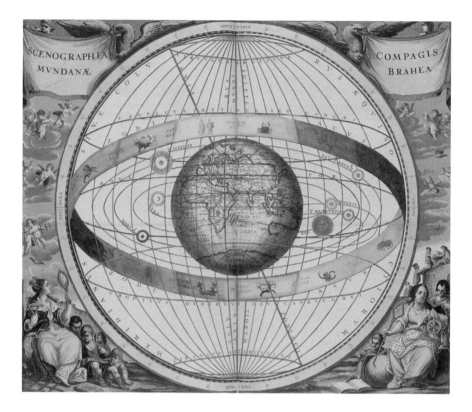

A 17th-century map depicts Tycho's belief that, while the sun revolves around Earth, the other planets orbit the sun.

Ursus had copied some of Tycho's original diagrams of the Tychonic model.

Ursus at first tried to deny the theft, but he eventually admitted it, telling Tycho, "It will teach you to look after your things more carefully in the future." Ursus even resorted to name-calling. He mocked Tycho's false nose and insulted Kirsten by pointing out that she and her husband had never been formally married. Tycho reacted by exposing Ursus' theft in public. As a result, Ursus' reputation was seriously damaged, and he died in disgrace in 1600.

Though Tycho had won a major battle regarding his theory, he had lost the war. The reactions of astronomers and other scholars to the Tychonic model were almost all negative. Like Copernicus' model, Tycho's model eliminated the idea of heavenly spheres. Most people were simply not ready to abandon the traditional views of the universe.

This experience frustrated and angered Tycho. He felt that other astronomers were still nothing more than "blind watchers of the sky." Of course, it is now clear that, as modern expert Rocky Kolb puts it, "Tycho shared in the blindness. His model was wrong." However, his years of hard work were not in vain. "This step in the wrong direction may have been necessary before the correct model could be developed." ❧

7 THE GREAT SKY SURVEY

Although the Tychonic model of the heavens turned out to be flawed, its creation produced something of lasting importance to astronomy. Tycho and his assistants compiled a massive, thorough collection of observations of the planets. Past astronomers, including Copernicus, had observed planetary motions, but they had studied these objects at selected points in their orbits. This provided little more than snapshots of their movements across the sky. In contrast, Tycho measured planetary motions week after week, month after month, for several years.

While Tycho was compiling the data about planetary motions, he saw a need to chart the positions of the stars. No one had made a complete map of the night sky since ancient times. In fact, astronomers

Astronomers have labeled 88 constellations that make up the night sky.

still sometimes used ancient star charts, even though they were widely recognized as inaccurate and unreliable.

In 1581, at the age of 34, Tycho launched a large-scale sky survey to chart the exact positions of up to 1,000 stars, an immense undertaking at the time. The work continued off and on throughout the decade, but the bulk of the data that ended up in the final catalog was collected between 1589 and 1591. In October 1590 alone, almost 400 stars were mapped. Tycho acted mainly as the supervisor of the project, overseeing a team of observers led by one of his most trusted assistants, Christian Longomontanus.

Tables of Sines, Tycho's book detailing his astronomical observations, is displayed alongside a telescope and another book by Copernicus at the University Library in Prague, Czech Republic.

Tycho and Longomontanus found that charting the brighter stars was easy. These were visible through holes in the sights of their instruments. In each case, the observer centered the star in the opening and recorded its exact position in the sky as quickly as possible since the star did not remain in the sight for very long. The stars appear to move across the sky each night because of Earth's daily rotation on its axis.

The fainter stars, by contrast, were a great deal harder to chart. In this pre-telescope era, each observer was completely dependent on the sharpness of his vision. The fainter the star, the more one's eye strained to see it. To make the faintest stars easier to study, the observers often widened the slits in their instrument sights. The drawback of this approach was that it was harder to estimate the center of a widened slit. So the positions of the fainter stars in Tycho's sky catalog tended to be less accurate than the positions of the brighter ones.

Much of the credit for Tycho's star catalog belongs to Danish mathematician and astronomer Christian Longomontanus (1562–1647). Longomontanus began attending the University of Copenhagen in 1588. Intelligent and hardworking, he impressed his teachers, and the following year they recommended him to Tycho. The young man worked for Tycho between 1589 and 1597 on Hven and again in 1600. In addition to his work on the star survey, Longomontanus tutored Tycho's sons. After Tycho's death, Longomontanus became a mathematics professor at the University of Copenhagen.

Still, the sky catalog was an important scientific achievement. The positioning of the brighter stars was significantly more accurate than on any prior star chart. In some cases, Tycho's readings were more precise than Copernicus' by nearly the width of the full moon. Tycho and his helpers also charted more stars than any other medieval astronomers. By the end of 1591, the catalog contained 777 stars, and Tycho and Longomontanus expanded it to about 1,000 in 1597. In

The accuracy of Tycho's star mapping depended on the brightness of each star.

number, that equaled the achieve-ment of the second-century Greek astronomer Claudius Ptolemy, who also charted roughly 1,000 stars. The difference was that Tycho's star positions were more accurate than Ptolemy's.

In 1597, while finishing his great star survey, Tycho and his family had to begin packing up their belongings. After more than 20 fruitful and happy years on Hven, Tycho felt he had no choice but to leave.

The events leading to this deci-sion began in 1588, the year Tycho

Claudius Ptolemy, who lived from about 100 to 178, was one of the leading astronomers of ancient times. One of his greatest achieve-ments was his book, Syntaxis, *now called* Almagest. *It included a catalog of the posi-tions of 1,022 stars in 48 constellations. This remained the foremost sky map in the world until Tycho published his own in the 1590s.*

had published his model of the heavens. Tycho's long-time friend and patron, King Frederick II, died that year. The king's 10-year-old son, Christian, ascended Denmark's throne as King Christian IV. Because of his age, King Christian was not allowed to exer-cise his full authority right away. For several years, members of the powerful royal council, the Rigsraad, ruled the country.

Most of these noblemen did not share Frederick's interest in science or his trust in Tycho Brahe. Over time, they steadily reduced Tycho's financial support. This frustrated and angered him. Though he was a

Four years after meeting with Tycho, Christian IV became old enough to rule Denmark on his own. Uninterested in astronomy, the king focused on strengthening his country's military power.

rich man, he badly needed this funding to support his ambitious work and his lifestyle on Hven. Tycho hoped to solve the problem by impressing the new king. In July 1592, Christian visited the island, where the astronomer entertained him and led him on a tour of the observatories. Tycho even gave his cherished brass sky globe to the young king as a gift.

But these efforts were in vain. As the years went by, relations between Tycho and Christian became increasingly strained. Tycho repeatedly asked for more money, and the tone of his letters to the king grew more and more arrogant. The astronomer dared to remind Christian that he, Tycho, was a national treasure who deserved nothing less than royal treatment. The king angrily responded:

> *[How dare you] not blush to act as if you were my equal. ... I expect from this day to be respected by you in a different manner if you are to find me a gracious lord and king.*

In Tycho's view, his country was no longer grateful for the important services he had rendered. So in 1597, he not only departed from Hven, but left Denmark altogether. With his wife, children, some servants, and perhaps his jester—the dwarf Jeppe—he spent the next two years wandering across Europe. Tycho eventually arrived in Prague, the chief city of Bohemia, now the Czech Republic. At the invitation of Rudolf II, emperor of Bohemia, Austria, and Hungary, Tycho became the imperial mathematician.

Tycho and Rudolf liked each other from their first meeting in July 1599. Tycho later recalled:

Tycho settled in Prague after traveling two years around Europe.

The emperor immediately called me over to him with a nod ... and when I approached him he graciously reached out his hand to me. ... [He said] how agreeable my arrival was for him and that he promised to support me and my research, all the while smiling in the most kindly way, so that his whole face beamed.

Deeply impressed by Tycho, Rudolf granted him an annual salary even larger than the one Frederick had paid him. In addition, the emperor helped Tycho establish a new observatory. It was built in a castle at Benatky and Jizerou, about 31 miles (50 km) from Prague. There Tycho began collecting quadrants and other astronomical instruments and hiring new assistants.

One of these assistants arrived at Benatky in February 1600. The man, a little-known mathematician at the time, was Johannes Kepler. Tycho was immediately impressed with Kepler's intelligence. "I love you very dearly on account of the excellent qualities of your mind," he told Kepler. Tycho had no way of knowing that his work with Kepler would eventually revolutionize humanity's view of the universe. ℘

King Rudolf II
(1552–1612)

8 A MYSTERIOUS DEATH

During the last year and a half of Tycho's life, he and his new assistant, Johannes Kepler, sought to solve the riddle of planetary motions. Were their orbits shaped like circles or some other shape? What laws governed their motions around the sun? They knew that the answers to these questions would reveal the nature of the heavens.

When Kepler first arrived at Tycho's new observatory in 1600, Tycho had only one quibble with his new assistant: Kepler supported the Copernican model of the heavens, in which Earth revolves around the sun, rather than the Tychonic model. Both men knew that there was a way to prove which theory was correct. Since Tycho had collected a mass of data about planetary motions over the course of two decades, they

Tycho Brahe and Johannes Kepler used quadrants to view the sky from the terrace of Belvedere Castle in Prague.

Kepler analyzed the planetary data and discussed the possibilities with Tycho.

hoped careful studies of this data would reveal the shapes of the planets' orbits and other vital information. This, in turn, would help future astronomers unveil the true structure of the planetary system.

Therefore, Tycho allowed Kepler to begin poring

over the data. The older man imposed one condition: He asked Kepler to promise that he would not reveal any of the data to anyone else. Kepler readily agreed and got to work.

As the months rolled by, Tycho found that Kepler was not an easy person to work with. Kepler was as stubborn and proud as Tycho. He demanded a separate house at Benatky for himself and his family. He also wanted Tycho to persuade Emperor Rudolf to provide him with a large salary. Despite Kepler's rudeness, Tycho repeatedly forgave him and kept him on as an assistant, probably because of Kepler's brilliance as a mathematician. Tycho persuaded Rudolf to grant Kepler an income. Tycho proposed that when the riddle of the planetary motions was solved, the information should be published as the *Rudolphine Tables*. Greatly flattered, Rudolf accepted the honor.

However, Tycho fell ill after attending a dinner party on October 13, 1601. Kepler later claimed that 54-year-old Tycho had had too much to drink, and

> *German mathematician and astronomer Johannes Kepler (1571–1630) was one of the giants of early modern science. In 1577, at age 5, Kepler was captivated by the same comet that Tycho studied at Uraniborg. In 1594, Kepler began teaching mathematics at Graz Seminary School in Austria. Five years later, Tycho summoned the younger man to Bohemia. After working with Tycho in 1600 and 1601, Kepler studied Tycho's planetary data for several years. He eventually formulated his three laws of planetary motion.*

though he badly needed to relieve himself, he felt it would be bad manners to leave the table. Therefore, he remained seated for hours. By the time he reached home, Kepler wrote, Tycho "could no longer urinate." For several days, Tycho suffered severe muscle cramps and could neither eat nor sleep. Finally, on October 24, "amid the prayers, tears, and efforts of his family to console him, his strength failed and he passed away very peacefully."

On November 4, Tycho's body was laid to rest in the Church of Our Lady Before Tyn in Prague. According to an eyewitness account:

> *The casket was draped with black cloth and decorated in gold with the Brahe coat of arms. ... The casket was borne by twelve imperial officials, all noblemen. Behind the casket walked Tycho's younger son ... followed by ... Tycho's assistants and servants, then Tycho's wife, guided by two distinguished old royal judges, and finally his ... daughters ... and after them the most distinguished citizens.*

For a long time, the cause of Tycho's death was recorded as uremia—a serious medical condition in which a person is unable to urinate, often because kidney stones create a blockage. The diagnosis began to arouse suspicion, however, after medical experts examined Tycho's remains in 1901. They

A carved tomb-stone depicting Tycho and his astronomical instruments marks his tomb at the Church of Our Lady Before Tyn.

could find no evidence of kidney stones or other kinds of blockage, but some surviving hairs from his beard were collected and placed in a jar for future study. In 1991, the hairs came into the possession of the Danish ambassador to the Czech Republic. He took them back to Denmark, and they ended up at the Institute of Forensic Medicine at the University of Copenhagen.

Researchers at the institute examined the hairs using the same medical devices used to solve modern crimes. They found that Tycho's hairs contained abnormally high levels of mercury. This indicated that Tycho had died of mercury poisoning, not uremia. Experts who examined the evidence pointed out that mercury poisoning and uremia can produce similar

Mercury, also known as quicksilver, is a naturally occurring, highly poisonous liquid metal.

symptoms. Since Tycho's doctors had heard about his urinary problems, it would have been easy for them to give the wrong diagnosis.

After learning that Tycho died of an overdose of mercury, modern scholars wanted to know how the metal got into his body. They thought he may have died from long-term, repeated exposure to liquid mercury. Since Tycho used mercury in some of his alchemy experiments, he may have breathed in mercury fumes in his lab. He may have handled the mercury with his hands as well. Either way, the deadly metal could have built up in his system over time, eventually killing him.

Mercury poisoning and uremia have a number of symptoms in common. Among them are nausea, vomiting, fever, fatigue, muscle cramps, loss of appetite, and mental depression. Since Tycho displayed most or all of these symptoms in the days before his death, it is not surprising that his doctors diagnosed his illness as uremia.

In 1996, after more sensitive tests were done on Tycho's hair, scientists ruled out the possibility of a fatal, long-term exposure. The new tests showed that Tycho had consumed a large dose of mercury within one or two days of his death. Therefore, any mercury he had been exposed to before that day might have made him sick, but it was a single fatal dose that killed him. Either the astronomer accidentally swallowed the fatal dose himself, or someone slipped it into his food or drink.

Since mercury was commonly used in alchemy experiments, an early theory of the cause of Tycho's death was an overexposure to his alchemy equipment.

Of the scholars that argue someone purposely poisoned Tycho, some suggest it was one or more members of the Bohemian government. Since the empire ruled by Rudolf II was officially Roman Catholic, Rudolf's Catholic government officials may have disliked his close relationship with Tycho, who was a Protestant.

Johannes Kepler is also sometimes mentioned as the culprit. Joshua and Anne-Lee Gilder summarize this theory in *Heavenly Intrigue*. They suggest that Kepler wanted to acquire Tycho's planetary data and get rid of Tycho in the process. Then Kepler would receive all the credit for developing the laws of planetary motion. Although this scenario is possible, the case against Kepler is mostly circumstantial. No concrete evidence has been found to prove that he killed his boss.

Many experts now think that Tycho accidentally overdosed on mercury. It was common in Tycho's time for people to put small amounts of mercury in medicines. They mistakenly thought that this would help reduce aches and pains. In Tycho's last days, as he suffered through severe cramps, it is quite possible that he would have used medicine traced with mercury to help relieve the pain. Still, it may be that the true manner of Tycho's mysterious death will never be known. ❧

9 An Important Legacy

Tycho Brahe was a legend in his own time, and he remains a legend today. For thousands of years, humans had observed the heavens using only their eyes, but Tycho was the last major astronomer to do so. A mere eight years after his death, Italian astronomer Galileo Galilei became the first scientist to point a telescope skyward and publish his findings, which revolutionized studies of the heavens.

Although Tycho had no telescope, he did have numerous astronomical instruments, many of his own design. Using these, he achieved a higher level of accuracy than anyone before him. The importance of using accurate instruments was not lost on his assistants. Tycho supported and trained dozens of younger researchers at his observatories over

Statues of Tycho were built throughout Europe to honor his contributions to astronomy.

> Italian scholar and astronomer Galileo Galilei (1564–1642) did not invent the telescope. That honor goes to Dutch spectacle makers. In 1608, they constructed a spyglass that used small lenses to magnify distant objects. Galileo, however, was one of the first astronomers to build his own telescope and to aim it at the sky. In November 1609, he saw craters and mountain chains on the moon. In January 1610, he discovered the four largest moons of the planet Jupiter. A new era in astronomy had dawned.

the years, and many of them later became leading scholars.

Christian Longomontanus, whose aid had been pivotal in compiling Tycho's star charts, became a renowned mathematics professor. Another of Tycho's assistants, Willem Blaeu, became a leading mapmaker. Paul Wittich and other assistants went on to design astronomical instruments. They built upon Tycho's instrument designs, adapting them to the new telescopic era. Like him, they dedicated themselves to attaining the most precise measurements possible.

Tycho also passed on to later astronomers his new and improved observational methods and practices. He showed that it was essential to study an object night after night, month after month, to create a complete picture of the object's movements. His successors took this lesson to heart, and long-term studies of the heavenly bodies became the norm in astronomy.

Tycho also rid science of the incorrect, traditional view of the universe. He refuted many of the old claims, which people had long accepted without question. In addition, Tycho's observations of the 1572 supernova and 1577 comet inspired him to create a new model of the heavens. The Tychonic model—which kept Earth at the center of all things—turned out to be wrong, but it took a step in the right direction, stating that most other heavenly bodies orbit the sun.

Tycho's charts of the stars and the planetary motions were used for reference by future astronomers.

Tycho's vision of the heavens enjoyed a brief period of acceptance after his death. Beginning in about 1620, a number of astronomers, especially those who worked for the pope in Rome, adopted the Tychonic model. They saw it as an acceptable alternative to the Copernican model. Tycho's scheme retained a central, unmoving Earth, and some church officials were simply not yet ready to embrace the sun-centered view given by Galileo and a growing number of scientists in the 1600s.

If Tycho had lived longer, he probably would have ended up agreeing with the views of Copernicus and Galileo. In fact, Tycho's data about the planets allowed Kepler to work out the laws of planetary motion. This eventually proved the correctness of the Copernican model.

Kepler's achievements—based on Tycho's data— began a mere two days after Tycho's death. Rudolf II needed someone to fill Tycho's post as imperial mathematician. The emperor gave Kepler the job and urged him to continue to try to solve the riddle of planetary movements.

Kepler knew he could not achieve this difficult goal without Tycho's planetary data, which now belonged to Tycho's family. Worried that Kirsten, Jorgen, and other heirs might be reluctant to part with the manuscripts, Kepler decided to steal them. He later admitted it, writing in a 1605 letter: "I confess

Rudolf II hired Kepler to continue Tycho's research of planetary motions.

that when Tycho died, I quickly took advantage of the [situation] by taking the observations under my care, or perhaps usurping [stealing] them."

At first, no one noticed that the manuscripts were missing. About a year later, Tycho's son-in-law, Frans Tengnagel, realized they were gone. He immediately suspected Kepler and demanded he give them back. Kepler did so, but Tengnagel soon realized that the information was useless without someone of Kepler's brilliance to study it. So Kepler was allowed to work

Tycho's manuscripts containing the planetary data passed through many hands following his death. First, Kepler took possession of them. After Kepler's death in 1630, his heirs inherited the manuscripts. In 1662, his son, Ludwig Kepler, sold them to Denmark's King Frederick III. Frederick gave them to the Royal Library in Copenhagen, where they remain today.

with the manuscripts again.

In 1609, after working with Tycho's observational data for years, Kepler published the first two of his three planetary laws. The first states that the planets travel in elliptical, or oval-shaped, orbits. He proved that the long-standing view that orbits were circular was wrong. The second law states that a planet increases in speed as it nears the sun and decreases in speed as it moves away from the sun. In 1619, Kepler published his third law, which showed a mathematical relationship between a planet's distance from the sun and how long it takes to orbit the sun.

These laws provided strong evidence that the Copernican model was correct. Also, the great English mathematician Isaac Newton (1643–1727) later used Kepler's laws to work out the theory of gravity. In this way, later generations of scientists continually built on Tycho's work.

These scientists did not forget the debt they owed Tycho. Kepler gave credit to his former mentor in the preface of his 1619 book *Harmony of the Worlds*. God had given humanity "the most diligent of

Tycho Brahe and Johannes Kepler, considered two of the greatest astronomers in history, were honored with a statue in Prague.

TYCHO BRAHE
JOHANNES KEPLER

observers, Tycho Brahe," Kepler wrote. "It is fitting that we accept with grateful minds this gift from God, and both acknowledge and build upon it. ... [This] will lead us along a path to the reform of the whole of Astronomy." ℘

95 ∽

BRAHE'S LIFE

1546

Born December 14 in Knudstrup, Denmark

1552

Begins attending elementary school at a church near his home

1560

Witnesses a partial eclipse of the sun, awakening his interest in astronomy

1560

1540

Spanish explorer Francisco Vasquez de Coronado leads an expedition into what is now the southwestern United States

1558

Elizabeth I is crowned in England, beginning a 45-year reign as queen

WORLD EVENTS

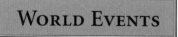

1562

Enters the University of Leipzig in Germany

1566

Enrolls at the University of Rostock, also in Germany

1571

Father dies; inherits a share of the family property in Knudstrup

1570

1564

Poet and playwright William Shakespeare is born

1570

The potato is introduced to Europe from South America

BRAHE'S LIFE

1572

Observes and studies a "new star" and determines that it lies far beyond the moon; begins living with Kirsten Jorgensdatter

1573

Publishes a book, *De Stella Nova*, describing the new star; daughter Kirstine is born

1576

Is given the island of Hven by King Frederick II; begins building a castle and observatory there; Kirstine dies

1575

1572

Scottish religious reformer and Presbyterian John Knox dies in Edinburgh

1576

English navigator Martin Frobisher, on his search for the Northwest Passage, enters the Canadian bay that now bears his name

WORLD EVENTS

1577

Sees and studies a bright comet and proves that it lies outside Earth's atmosphere; son Claus is born

1580

Constructs a large brass sky globe, part of a growing collection of advanced astronomical instruments

1581

Completes the observatory, called Uraniborg

1580

1577

Francis Drake sails around the world by way of Cape Horn

1582

Pope Gregory XIII invents a calendar that more closely follows the seasonal year than the Julian calendar currently in use

BRAHE'S LIFE

1585

Son Jorgen is born

1588

Publishes *Concerning the New Phenomena of the Ethereal World*, in which he introduces his model of the heavens; King Frederick dies

1597

Leaves Denmark after a falling out with Frederick's successor, King Christian IV

1590

1587

Virginia Dare is born on Roanoke Island off the coast of North Carolina to become the first child born of English parents in North America

1597

The world's first opera is performed in Florence, Italy

WORLD EVENTS

1599

Settles in Bohemia (now the Czech Republic)

1600

Begins working with Johannes Kepler, who will later use Tycho's data to explain the motions of the planets

1601

Dies October 24 in Bohemia

1600

1599

Lord Chamberlain's company builds the Globe theater in Southwark, London, where Shakespeare's plays are performed

1603

James I becomes king of England and Ireland

DATE OF BIRTH: December 14, 1546

BIRTHPLACE: Knudstrup, Denmark

FATHER: Otte Brahe (1518–1571)

MOTHER: Beate Bille (1526–1605)

EDUCATION: University of Copenhagen, University of Leipzig, University of Rostock

SPOUSE: Kirsten Jorgensdatter (?–1604)

DATE OF MARRIAGE: Not formally married

CHILDREN: Kirstine (1573–1576)
Magdalene (1574–1620)
Claus (1577–1577)
Sophie (1578–1646)
Elisabeth (1579–1613)
Cecile (1580–1640)
Tycho (1581–1627)
Jorgen (1585–1661)

DATE OF DEATH: October 24, 1601

PLACE OF BURIAL: Prague, Bohemia (now the Czech Republic)

FURTHER READING

Boerst, William J. *Tycho Brahe: Mapping the Heavens.* Greensboro, N.C.: Morgan Reynolds Pub., 2003.

Gow, Mary. *Tycho Brahe: Astronomer.* Berkeley Heights, N.J.: Enslow Publishers, 2002.

Solway, Andrew. *Quantum Leaps and Big Bangs!: A History of Astronomy.* Chicago: Heinemann Library, 2006.

Voelkel, James R. *Johannes Kepler and the New Astronomy.* New York: Oxford University Press, 1999.

LOOK FOR MORE SIGNATURE LIVES BOOKS ABOUT THIS ERA:

Nicolaus Copernicus: *Father of Modern Astronomy*

Galileo: *Astronomer and Physicist*

Robert Hooke: *Natural Philosopher and Scientific Explorer*

Gerardus Mercator: *Father of Modern Mapmaking*

Sir Isaac Newton: *Brilliant Mathematician and Scientist*

On the Web

For more information on this topic, use FactHound.

1. Go to *www.facthound.com*
2. Type in this book ID: 0756533090
3. Click on the *Fetch It* button.

FactHound will find the best Web sites for you.

Historic Sites

Tycho Brahe Museum at Ven (Hven)
Former All Saints Church
Ven, Sweden
46 418 470 582
Exhibits about Tycho's life and accomplishments and replicas of several of his astronomical instruments

Church of Our Lady Before Tyn
Old Town Square
Old Town, Prague 1
Czech Republic
420 222 318 186
Tycho's tomb and a memorial to him

aristocrats
members of the upper class

armillary
astronomical device, consisting of a framework of metal rings, that shows the positions of stars and planets in the sky

celestial
having to do with the sky or heavens

constellation
group of stars that seem to form a pattern in the sky

cosmic
having to do with the heavens or universe

courtier
member of the royal court of a king or queen

Muses
group of ancient Greek goddesses who oversaw the arts and sciences

parallax
the apparent movement of an object against a background caused by the observer's own movement

quadrants
instruments for measuring the altitude of stars above the horizon

radius
device shaped like a cross used to measure the positions of stars; also known as a cross staff

uremia
medical condition in which a person is unable to urinate; over time, toxins (poisons) in the urine back up into the bloodstream, causing illness

Chapter 1

Page 10, line 9: "SN 1572: Tycho's Supernova." Students for the Exploration and Development of Space. 7 Dec. 2006. www.seds.org/~spider/spider/Vars/sn1572.html

Page 11, line 4: Ibid.

Page 16, line 2: Ibid.

Page 17, line 11: Rocky Kolb. *Blind Watchers of the Sky: The People and Ideas That Shaped Our View of the Universe.* New York: Helix, 1997, p. 19.

Page 17, line 17: Victor E. Thoren. *The Lord of Uraniborg: A Biography of Tycho Brahe.* New York: Cambridge University Press, 1990, p. 72.

Chapter 2

Page 21, line 12: *The Lord of Uraniborg*, p. 4.

Page 21, line 26: Ibid.

Page 22, line 7: Ibid., p. 9.

Page 22, line 16: Ibid.

Page 24, line 10: Ibid., p. 16.

Page 26, line 7: Johan Runeberg. "Tycho Brahe and Uraniborg." 11 April 2000. 7 Dec. 2006. www.hven.net/EUBORG2.html

Chapter 3

Page 32, line 19: *The Lord of Uraniborg*, p. 23.

Page 36, line 3: Ibid., pp. 36–37.

Chapter 4

Page 40, line 17: Ibid., p. 104.

Page 43, line 1: John R. Christianson. *On Tycho's Island: Tycho Brahe and His Assistants, 1570–1601.* New York: Cambridge University Press, 2000, pp. 22–23.

Page 43, sidebar: Marjorie Rowling. *Everyday Life in Medieval Times.* New York: Putnam, 1968, p. 105.

Page 47, line 1: *On Tycho's Island: Tycho Brahe and His Assistants, 1570–1601*, p. 296.

Chapter 5

Page 50, line 4: *The Lord of Uraniborg*, p. 146.

Page 56, line 3: Ibid., p. 183.

Page 57, line 10: Ibid., p. 184.

Chapter 6

Page 60, line 10: *Blind Watchers of the Sky*, p. 31.

Page 60, sidebar: *Everyday Life in Medieval Times*, p. 203.

Page 64, line 11: Ibid., p. 32.

Page 66, line 4: *The Lord of Uraniborg*, p. 393.

Page 67, line 3: *Blind Watchers of the Sky*, p. 36.

Chapter 7

Page 75, line 11: Ibid., p. 37.

Page 76, line 1: *The Lord of Uraniborg*, p. 412.

Page 77, line 20: Ibid., p. 436.

Chapter 8

Page 82, line 4: Ibid., p. 469.

Page 82, line 13: Ibid., pp. 469–470.

Chapter 9

Page 92, line 28: "Johannes Kepler." *Northwestern University*. 8 Dec. 2006.
www.physics.northwestern.edu/Phyx103/web/kepler.html

Page 94, line 28: J.V. Field. "Quotations by Johannes Kepler." JOC/EFR.
November 2003. 8 Dec. 2006. www.gap-system.org/~history/Quotations/
Kepler.html

Aaboe, Asger. *Episodes from the Early History of Astronomy.* New York: Springer, 2001.

Beatty, J. Kelly, et al., eds. *The New Solar System.* 4th ed. New York: Sky Pub., 1999.

Christianson, John R. *On Tycho's Island: Tycho Brahe and His Assistants, 1570–1601.* New York: Cambridge University Press, 2000.

Ferguson, Kitty. *Tycho & Kepler: The Unlikely Partnership That Forever Changed Our Understanding of the Heavens.* New York: Walker & Co., 2002.

Field, J.V. "Quotations by Johannes Kepler." JOC/EFR. November 2003. 8 Dec. 2006. www.gap-system.org/~history/Quotations/Kepler.html

Gilder, Joshua, and Anne-Lee Gilder. *Heavenly Intrigue: Johannes Kepler, Tycho Brahe, and the Murder Behind One of History's Greatest Scientific Discoveries.* New York: Doubleday, 2004.

Hoskin, Michael, ed. *The Cambridge Concise History of Astronomy.* New York: Cambridge University Press, 1999.

"Johannes Kepler." Northwestern University. 8 Dec. 2006. www.physics.northwestern.edu/Phyx103/web/kepler.html

Kepler, Johannes. *Harmonies of the World.* Ed. Stephen Hawking. Philadelphia: Running Press, 2005.

Kolb, Rocky. *Blind Watchers of the Sky: The People and Ideas That Shaped Our View of the Universe.* New York: Helix, 1997.

Rowling, Marjorie. *Everyday Life in Medieval Times.* New York: Putnam, 1968.

Runeberg, Johan. "Tycho Brahe and Uraniborg." 11 April 2000. 7 Dec. 2006. www.hven.net/EUBORG2.html

"SN 1572: Tycho's Supernova." Students for the Exploration and Development of Space. 7 Dec. 2006. www.seds.org/~spider/spider/Vars/sn1572.html

Thoren, Victor E. *The Lord of Uraniborg: A Biography of Tycho Brahe.* New York: Cambridge University Press, 1990.

In addition to his acclaimed volumes on ancient civilizations, historian Don Nardo has published several studies of scientific discoveries and phenomena, as well as scientists. Nardo lives with his wife, Christine, in Massachusetts.

Image Credits